OLDFANGLED
DISCOURTESY

OLDFANGLED DISCOURTESY

A REPOSITORY OF CONTUMELIOUS LOCUTION

BY **LEONARD APPLE** ESQ.

FOR YOUR EDIFICATION AND MERRIMENT

CONTENTS

Introduction

Welcome to the world of old-fashioned insulting words! This book will take you on a journey through the fascinating and often hilarious world of old-fashioned insults. From the hilarious to the downright offensive, you'll learn about words that were commonly used in the past to express disapproval, contempt, or indignation.

In today's world, people are more careful with their words, and the use of insulting language is often frowned upon. However, this was not always the case, and throughout history, people have used language to insult, mock and belittle others. In fact, there was a time when using insulting words was considered a skill, and people would compete to come up with the wittiest and most cutting insults. In this book, we will explore the world of old-fashioned insulting words, where language was used as a weapon, and a quick tongue was an asset.

The art of insult dates to ancient times when the Greek and Roman philosophers used verbal jousting as a form of debate. The ability to insult your opponent was seen as a sign of intelligence and wit. The ancient Greeks had a word for this form of insult, "sarcasm," which means to tear flesh. The Romans had a similar concept known as "contumely," which was a verbal attack intended to humiliate the target.

Throughout history, insulting words have been used for a variety of reasons. In some cases, they were used as a means of asserting dominance or to put others in their place. In other cases, they were used to express frustration or anger. Some insults were directed at specific groups of people, such as women or minorities, while others were directed at individuals based on their perceived weaknesses or flaws.

In the Middle Ages, insults were often used to settle disputes or as a form of entertainment. Duelling insults were a popular pastime among knights and courtiers. In fact, some of the most famous insults in history were exchanged during duels. For example, during a duel between the English playwright and poet, William Shakespeare, and the playwright Robert Greene, Greene referred to Shakespeare as a "shake-scene," a derogatory term for an actor. In response, Shakespeare referred to Greene as "an upstart crow."

Insults were also used in literature, particularly in the works of Shakespeare. In his plays, Shakespeare used insults as a way of revealing character and creating conflict. His insults were often poetic and cleverly constructed, and they are still studied and admired today:

"Thou art a boil, a plague sore."

"I do desire we may be better strangers."

"Thou cream-faced loon!"

"Thou art a base, proud, shallow, beggarly, three-suited, hundred-pound, filthy worsted-stocking knave."

"Thou art a tedious fool."

"Thou art a natural coward without instinct."

"Thou art a flesh-monger, a fool, and a coward."

"I scorn you, scurvy companion."

"Thou art as loathsome as a toad."

"Thou lump of foul deformity!"

During the 18th and 19th centuries, insulting words became more refined and sophisticated. The art of insult became a popular pastime among the aristocracy, who competed to see who could come up with the wittiest and most clever insults. Insults were also used as a means of social control, particularly among women. Women who were seen as too outspoken or independent were often subjected to verbal attacks to bring them back into line.

In the 20th century, insulting words took on a different character. With the rise of mass media, insults became more widespread and less sophisticated. Insults were used to sell products, to attract attention, and to create controversy. In politics, insults were used as a way of discrediting opponents and rallying support. The use of insults became so prevalent that many people became desensitized to them, and they were no longer seen as a sign of wit or intelligence.

Today, insulting words are still used, but they are often seen as crude and offensive. Many people believe that insults have no place in polite society, and they are quick to condemn anyone who uses them. However, there are still those who believe that the art of insult has value. They argue that insults can be used to express frustration or anger, and that they can be a way of asserting oneself in a world where power dynamics are often unfair.

Throughout the book, we will provide examples of old-fashioned insulting words and their meanings and origins. We will explore insults that were once commonly used but have fallen out of use.

This book is not intended to encourage or condone the use of insulting words. Instead, it is intended to be a study of a cultural phenomenon that has been a part of human history for thousands of years. We hope that this book will not only entertain but also educate readers on this often-overlooked aspect of human culture.

mooncalf

[moon-kaf, -kahf]

noun

DESCRIPTION:
A dreamer, someone absent-minded
or distracted; a fool, simpleton.

ORIGIN: *From moon + calf, after
a superstition that the moon caused
abnormal fetal development.*

'Only a mooncalf, with a porridge-bowl instead of a head, could have mistaken these remarks.' 5

jobbernowl

[job-ber-nowl]

noun

DESCRIPTION:
A stupid person; a blockhead:

 ORIGIN: *Middle English, compare French jobard ("gullible, crazy") and noll ("head").*

'That he pays not the least regard
o the requirements of convention
narks him out as either a superior
oul or a rightdown jobbernowl."

7

lunkhead

[luhngk-hed]

noun

DESCRIPTION:
a dull or stupid person; blockhead.

ORIGIN: *1850–55, Americanism; lunk (perhaps blend of lump and hunk) + head.*

"Why, you lunkhead, this gentleman
will tell you I am his guest!"

nincompoop

[nin-kuh-m-poop, ning-]

noun

DESCRIPTION:
a fool or simpleton.

ORIGIN: *First recorded in 1670–80; origin uncertain.*

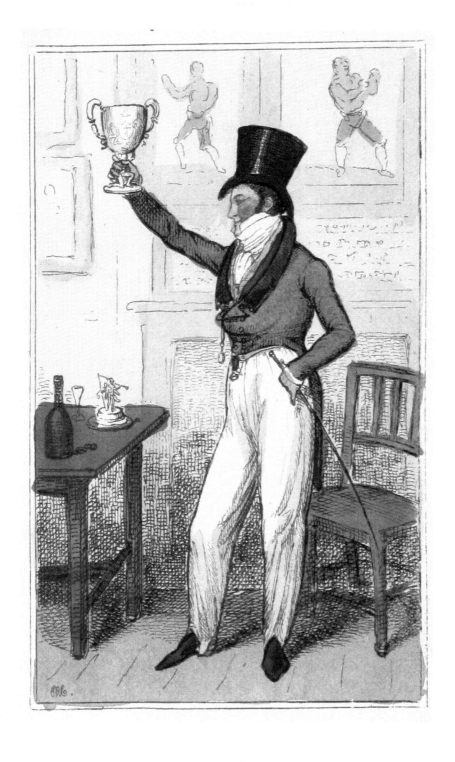

'When ye hear of a man a woman hez
nade, ye hears of a nincompoop.'

11

doodle

[dood-l]

noun

DESCRIPTION:
A fool, a simpleton, a mindless person.

ORIGIN: *First appeared in the early 17th century. German variants of the etymon include Dudeltopf, Dudentopf, Dudenkopf, Dude and Dödel.*

'Weep on! weep on! thou flouted loon,
Weep on! weep on! thou gowky doodle!"

jackanapes

[jak-uh-neyps]

noun

DESCRIPTION:
An impudent or mischievous person.

 ORIGIN: *1450, from "Jack of Naples", with "of Naples" rendered "a Napes" in vernacular.*

"I'd hate to say anything good about that
ong-winded jackanapes, but he does
now the short way to start a war."

15

numps

[nuhmps]

noun

DESCRIPTION:
A dolt; a blockhead.

ORIGIN: *Late 16th century; earliest use found in Thomas Nashe (d. c1601), writer. Origin uncertain.*

Actieuse NACHT-WIND-Zanger met zyn Tover Slons

Van de Haane
Quam 't van daane

ô de Tover-Lantaarn

2

'These are villainous engines indeed; but
ake heart, numps! here is not a word of
he stocks; and you need never stand in
we of any more honourable correction."

flapdoodle

[flap-dood-l]

noun

DESCRIPTION:
A speaker or writer of nonsense.

ORIGIN: *mid 19th century: an arbitrary formation.*

"This flapdoodle has written over four
hundred pages of mystical nonsense"

hooey

[hoo-ee]

noun

DESCRIPTION:
Silly or worthless talk, writing,
ideas, etc.; nonsense;

ORIGIN: *An Americanism dating
back to 1920–25; origin uncertain.*

'That's a lot of hooey and you know it!"

horsefeathers

[hawrs-feth-erz]

noun

DESCRIPTION:
Nonsense; indicates disbelief.

ORIGIN: *1925–30, Americanism; horse + feathers, as euphemism for horsemuck.*

"The story turned out to be such
a load of horsefeathers!"

moonshine

[moon-shahyn]

noun

DESCRIPTION:
Empty or foolish talk,
ideas, etc.; nonsense.

ORIGIN: *Late Middle English: moonlight.*

"Everything they said was just
a load of moonshine."

humbug

[huhm-buhg]

noun

DESCRIPTION:
A willfully false, deceptive,
or insincere person

ORIGIN: *First recorded in*
1730–40; origin uncertain.

'He was a tall, good-looking fellow enough;
 but if ever there was a humbug in the shape
 of a groom, Alfred Smirk was the man."

27

taradiddle

[tar-uh-did-l]

noun

DESCRIPTION:
Pretentious nonsense.

 ORIGIN: *First recorded in 1790– 1800; origin uncertain.*

"We would like to do so, of course; but
our sense of truth revolts against the
enunciation of such a taradiddle."

29

tommyrot

[tom-ee-rot]

noun

DESCRIPTION:
Nonsense; utter foolishness.

ORIGIN: *1880–85; tommy simpleton + rot*

'I am a young man still, with years
and years before me in which I shall
no doubt talk a lot of tommyrot."

trumpery

[truhm-puh-ree]

noun

DESCRIPTION:
Something without use or value;
rubbish; trash; worthless stuff.

ORIGIN: *1425–75; late Middle
English trompery deceit.*

'We can't afford to bring up fine ladies and
each them French and other trumpery."

33

fiddle-faddle

[fid-l-fad-l]

noun

DESCRIPTION:
Something trivial.

ORIGIN: *First recorded in 1570–80; gradational compound based on fiddle.*

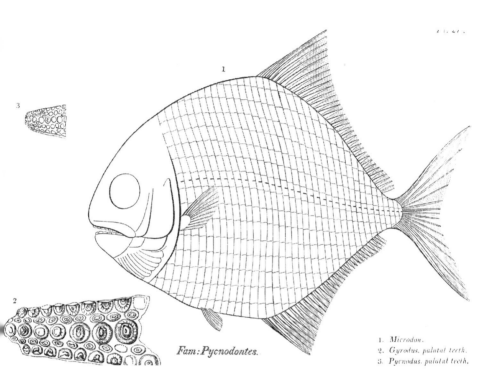

Fam : Pycnodontes.

1. Microdon.
2. Gyrodus. palatal teeth.
3. Pycnodus. palatal teeth.

'He said one day to me, "Why don't you
give up your fiddle-faddle of geology and
zoology, and turn to the occult sciences!"'

35

blatherskite

[blath-er-skahyt]

noun

DESCRIPTION:
A person given to voluble, empty talk.

ORIGIN: *1640–50; blather + skite.*

'The Confederate Major was of the
class referred to in polite American
parlance, as a "blatherskite."'

bosh

[bosh]

noun

DESCRIPTION:
Absurd or foolish talk; nonsense.

ORIGIN: *1830–35; Borrowed from Turkish; popularized from its use by British author James J. Morier (1780–1849).*

"Why, it's absolute bosh from
beginning to end.'"

buncombe

[buhng-kuh m]

noun

DESCRIPTION:
Insincere talk; claptrap; humbug.

ORIGIN: *Americanism; after speech in 16th Congress, 1819–21, by F. Walker, who said he was bound to speak for Buncombe (N.C. county in district he represented).*

"This is the surest way to fetch him;
ιe never fails to swell out his chest
νhen he hears that buncombe."

folderol

[fol-duh-rol]

noun

DESCRIPTION:
A useless ornament or accessory

ORIGIN: *Originally a nonsense refrain in old songs, used to make the song longer.*

"He [...] wouldn't have bought any of those foolish, foreign fandangles and folderols if he did have the money to waste."

43

nerts

[nurts]

interjection

DESCRIPTION:
Expression of dismay.

ORIGIN: *First recorded in 1930–35;*
Alteration of nuts, to avoid vulgar nuts.

"She wonders what he thought when she said, 'Oh, nerts!' after a bad shot."

gawky

[gaw-kee]

adjective

DESCRIPTION:
awkward; ungainly; clumsy.

ORIGIN: *First recorded in 1715–25.*

"A gawky farmer seized the boy and truck him cruelly across the mouth."

47

vassal

[vas-uh l]

noun

DESCRIPTION:
a servant or slave.

ORIGIN: *1300–50; Middle English*
< Middle French < Medieval Latin
vassallus, equivalent to vass(us) servant.

""Vassal am I to the youth up yonder," the gilla made answer."

dog

[dawg, dog]

noun

DESCRIPTION:
Someone who is morally reprehensible.

ORIGIN: *before 1050; Middle English dogge, Old English docga.*

"What is thy servant, which is but a dog,
that he should do this great thing?"

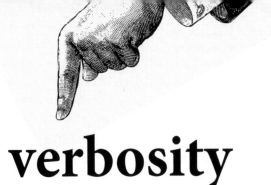

verbosity

[ver-bos-i-tee]

noun

DESCRIPTION:
The excess use of words, especially using more than are needed for clarity or precision; long-windedness.

ORIGIN: *From Middle French verbosité, from Late Latin verbositas, from Latin verbosus, from verbum ("the word").*

"Their capacity for talking so much
and saying so little is astonishing.
Their verbosity is unpalatable."

diffuse

[dih-fyoos]

adjective

DESCRIPTION:
characterized by great length
or discursiveness in speech
or writing; wordy.

ORIGIN: *1350–1400; Middle English.*

"The solution may have been too
diffuse to detect in his speech."

stolid

[stol-id]

adjective

DESCRIPTION:
not easily stirred or moved mentally;
unemotional; impassive.

ORIGIN: *First recorded in 1590–1600,*
stolid is from the Latin word stolidus.

"He was of a temper too stolid and sensible to vaste his time on random treasure hunting."

recalcitrant

[ri-kal-si-truhnt]

adjective

DESCRIPTION:
hard to deal with, manage, or operate.

ORIGIN: *Borrowed from French récalcitrant, from Latin ("be disobedient, kick back [as a horse]"), from calx ("heel"), 1820s.*

"His nimble fancy was recalcitrant
o mental discipline."

toady

[toh-dee]

noun

DESCRIPTION:
a sycophant who flatters others
to gain personal advantage.

ORIGIN: *First recorded in 1680–90.*

"Go on, Hiram, show 'em what you can do," urged
Luke Fodick, who was a sort of toady to Hiram
Shell, the school bully, if ever there was one."

flip-flop

[flip-flop]

verb

DESCRIPTION:
To alternate back and forth
between directly opposite
opinions, ideas, or decisions.

ORIGIN: *First recorded in 1655–65.*

"He claimed that the king had flip-flopped on certain issues."

gasbag

[gas-bag]

noun

DESCRIPTION:
Slang. a talkative, boastful
person; windbag.

ORIGIN: *First recorded in 1820–30.*

"First comes the typical Russian gasbag,
who talks and then talks some more."

choctaw

[chok-taw]

noun

DESCRIPTION:
something unintelligible, as
speech, illegible handwriting, or an
ineffectual explanation; gibberish:

ORIGIN: *First recorded in 1722.*

"*My best efforts at clarity were choctaw to him.*"   **67**

stool-pigeon

[stool pij-uh n]

noun

DESCRIPTION:
Slang. a person employed or
acting as a decoy or informer,
especially for the police.

ORIGIN: *An Americanism
dating back to 1820–30.*

"Now, the stool-pigeon in this trick
is a swell English crook."

wanton

[won-tn]

adjective

DESCRIPTION:
sexually lawless or unrestrained;
loose; lascivious; lewd.

ORIGIN: *1250–1300; Middle English
wantowen literally, undisciplined, ill-reared*

"Nuptial love maketh mankind; friendly
love perfecteth it; but wanton love
corrupteth, and embaseth it."

jabber

[jab-er]

noun

DESCRIPTION:
rapid, indistinct, or nonsensical
talk; gibberish.

ORIGIN: *1490–1500; apparently imitative*

"They differ from their brothers, because they
use a Sort of a Jabber, and do not go naked."

73

gab

 [gab]

noun

DESCRIPTION:
idle talk; chatter.

 ORIGIN: *1780–90; apparently expressive variant of gob.*

'Your French gab may be foul
with oaths for all I know."

barnyard

[bahrn-yahrd]

adjective

DESCRIPTION:
indecent; smutty; vulgar.

ORIGIN: *First recorded in 1505–15.*

"His barnyard humor made us all blush."

persuadable

[per-sweyd uh-buhl]

adjective

DESCRIPTION:
easily persuaded, convinced
or manipulated

ORIGIN: *From Latin, dating
back to 1505–15.*

"I dare say he did, for my master was
as persuadable as a woman, though
he'd fly out a bit sometimes at first."

snooty

[snoo-tee]

adjective

DESCRIPTION:
pompous; snobbish; inclined
to turn up one's nose.

ORIGIN: *First recorded in 1915–20.*

"Sir Sydney was an arrogant,
nooty, bigoted prig."

pantywaist

[pan-tee-weyst]

noun

DESCRIPTION:
Informal. a weak, effeminate man; sissy.

ORIGIN: *First recorded in 1925–30.*

"His rough, burly father was mortified
by the lad's pantywaist behavior."

slipshod

[slip-shod]

adjective

DESCRIPTION:
careless, untidy, or slovenly.

ORIGIN: *First recorded in 1570–80.*

"Mrs. Tucker was not a neat woman, and
everything looked neglected and slipshod."

85

insensate

[in-sen-seyt, -sit]

adjective

DESCRIPTION:
without human feeling or
sensitivity; cold; cruel; brutal.

ORIGIN: *First recorded in 1510–20.*

"He was known as a little demon, of
nsensate cruelty and viciousness."

gabby

[gab-ee]

adjective

DESCRIPTION:
Inclined to talk too much,
especially about trivia.

ORIGIN: *First recorded in 1710–20.*

"She was a gabby old lady, devoid of mirth."

pinhead

[pin-hed]

noun

DESCRIPTION:
a stupid person; nitwit.

 ORIGIN: *First recorded in 1655–65.*

"My sister is attracted to men who are pinheads." **91**

clodpate

[klod-peyt]

noun

DESCRIPTION:
A blockhead; a dolt or fool.

ORIGIN: *Old English clod- lump;*
related to cloud; pate- the head

"It was that he was a clodpate, and had no
dea of the absurdity that he was committing." 93

tumefied

 [too-muh-fahyd, tyoo-]

verb

DESCRIPTION:
ostentatiously lofty or high-flown

 ORIGIN: *First recorded in 1590–1600.*

Femme qui tense sans raison,
Ne fait quennij a la matson.

"She has no sentiment beyond a dudish
and tumefied admiration for herself,
and she covets every hen she sees."

insolent

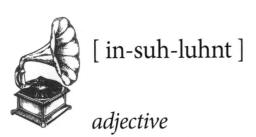

[in-suh-luhnt]

adjective

DESCRIPTION:
boldly rude or disrespectful;
contemptuously impertinent; insulting.

ORIGIN: *1350–1400; Middle English.*

"Their very posture—the way they loitered
and leaned and lolled about—was insolent."

97

fawning

[fawn-ing]

verb

DESCRIPTION:
Seeking favor by way of flattery

ORIGIN: *before 1000; Middle English fawnen, Old English fagnian, variant of fægnian to rejoice, make glad, derivative of fægen happy;*

"How like a fawning publican he looks!"

squander

[skwon-der]

noun

DESCRIPTION:
extravagant or wasteful expenditure

ORIGIN: *First recorded in 1585–95; origin uncertain*

"His successor and namesake did his best to squander away his fortune of thirty thousand pounds a year."

circumlocutory

[sur-kuhm-lok-yuh-tawr-ee, -tohr-ee]

noun

DESCRIPTION:
roundabout or indirect way of
speaking; the use of more words
than necessary to express an idea.

ORIGIN: *1375–1425; late Middle English*

"Herbert has a circumlocutory manner
over the phone which irritates me."

tony

[toh-nee]

adjective

DESCRIPTION:
characterized by or given to
pretentious or conspicuous show
in an attempt to impress others

ORIGIN: *An Americanism*
dating back to 1875–80

"Harriet was "tony" because she walked
with her elbows in and her head up."

quarrelsome

[kwawr-uh_l-suh_m, kwor-]

adjective

DESCRIPTION:
inclined to quarrel;
argumentative; contentious.

ORIGIN: *First recorded in 1590–1600*

"They are a quarrelsome lot and their captain has a proud stomach."

pleonasm

[plee-uh-naz-uh_m]

noun

DESCRIPTION:
the use of more words than are necessary
to express an idea; redundancy.

ORIGIN: *First recorded in 1580–90*

"*Nothing is gained in strength nor precision by this kind of pleonasm.*" **109**

recrementitious

[rek-ruh-men-tish-uh_s]

adjective

DESCRIPTION:
of, relating to, or consisting of
recrement or waste matter

ORIGIN: *First recorded in 1720–30*

"The narrative drags under the burden of recrementitious detail; and the story may deserve to be called dull at times."

fathead

[fat-hed]

noun

DESCRIPTION:
a stupid person; fool.

 ORIGIN: *First recorded in 1830–40*

"*Think of what every fathead princeling and beer-swilling ritter from here to Basel would say!*"

113

ostentatious

[os-ten-tey-shuh_s, -tuh_n-]

adjective

DESCRIPTION:
(of actions, manner, qualities exhibited, etc.) intended to attract notice

ORIGIN: *First recorded in 1650–60*

"There was an ostentatious pretension
in the "get up" of this gentleman."

recalcitrate

[ri-kal-si-treyt]

verb

DESCRIPTION:
to resist or oppose; show strong
objection or repugnance.

ORIGIN: *First recorded in 1615–25*

"Still there are some left who recalcitrate pertinaciously, clinging convulsively with hands and feet to their old ignorance."

grody

[groh-dee]

adjective

DESCRIPTION:
inferior in character or
quality; seedy; sleazy

ORIGIN: *1960–65, Americanism;
probably alteration of grotesque*

"They lived for a month in a grody little
shack without lights or running water."

nix

[niks]

Interjection

DESCRIPTION:
A warning cry when a policeman
etc. was sighted in the street.

ORIGIN: *1780–90; < German:
variant of nichts nothing*

"_"Nix!" she exclaimed to her friends_
as they attempted to leave school
early. "The principal sees us!""

quack

[kwak]

noun

DESCRIPTION:
a person who pretends, professionally
or publicly, to skill, knowledge,
or qualifications he or she does
not possess; a charlatan.

ORIGIN: *First recorded in 1620–
30; short for quacksalver*

"So a French quack adorns his shop
with a gilded bust of Hippocrates!"

coiner

[koi-ner]

noun

DESCRIPTION:
A person who invents or
fabricates (stories, lies, etc.).

ORIGIN: *From Middle English*
coynour, from Middle French
coigneur; equivalent to coin +_ -er.

"*The truth is, men in generall hate lying, both the coiner of it, and the teller of it [...]*"

eyewash

[ahy-wosh, ahy-wawsh]

noun

DESCRIPTION:
Informal. nonsense; bunk.

ORIGIN: *First recorded in 1865–70*

DEBATE AND ORATORY

"All the high-sounding arguments
for a moral world and all the laws
on the books implementing those
arguments are just eyewash."

bush-league

[boo_sh-leeg]

adjective

DESCRIPTION:
inferior or amateurish; mediocre:

ORIGIN: *An Americanism dating back to 1905–10*

"Neither is it some bush-league Johnny-
come-lately gathering with C-list
speakers and a shoe-string budget."

129

retrograde

[re-truh-greyd]

adjective

DESCRIPTION:
Archaic. contrary; opposed.

ORIGIN: *1350–1400; Middle English*

"Once in a private debate she referred
to him as a "learned barbarian
and a retrograde medivalist.""

wimp

[wimp]

adjective

DESCRIPTION:
a weak, ineffectual, timid person.

ORIGIN: *1915–20, Americanism;*
origin uncertain

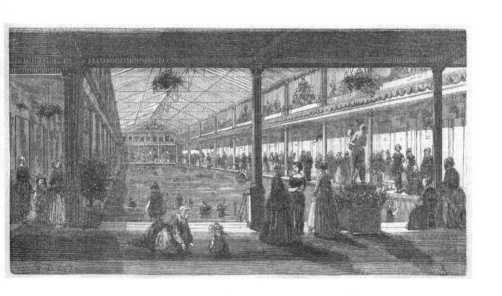

""The men here are wimps," the hotel
receptionist said scornfully."

baloney

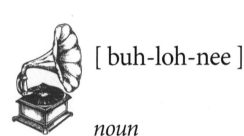

[buh-loh-nee]

noun

DESCRIPTION:
Slang. foolishness; nonsense.

ORIGIN: *1915–20, Americanism;*

"The hypocrisy here is monumental, even by traditional foreign-policy standards of baloney." 135

sophist

[sof-ist]

noun

DESCRIPTION:
One who is misleading or
deceptive in argument.

ORIGIN: *1535–45; < Latin sophista*

"*The one acts like a sophist, the other like a true man of genius.*"

stonewall

[stohn-wawl]

verb

DESCRIPTION:
Informal. to block, stall, or
resist intentionally

ORIGIN: *From Middle English*
stonwal, stone wall, stanewalle
("wall made of stone")

"When husbands stonewall, remember,
it triggers flooding in their wives,
who feel completely stymied."

139

bumpkin

[buhmp-kin]

noun

DESCRIPTION:
an awkward, simple, unsophisticated
person from a rural area; yokel.

ORIGIN: *1560–70; < Middle Dutch
bommekijn "little barrel," equivalent
to boom beam + -kijn -kin*

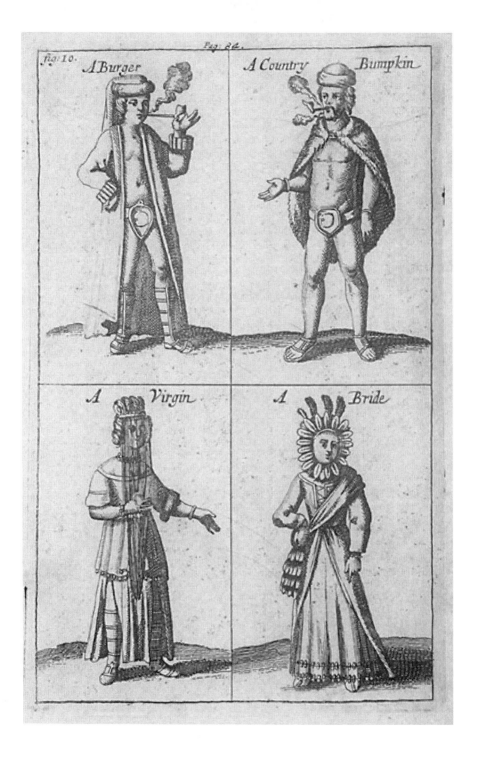

"There was little to be done in diplomacy
with a bumpkin like that."

imbecile

[im-buh-sil, -suh_l or,
esp. British, -seel]

noun

DESCRIPTION:
Informal. a dunce; blockhead; dolt:

ORIGIN: *1540–50; earlier imbecill <
Latin imb_cillus weak; -ile replacing
-ill by confusion with suffix -ile*

"The family was descended from a
Revolutionary soldier, who had an
illegitimate feeble-minded son by
an imbecile young woman."

bovine

 [boh-vahyn, -vin, -veen]

adjective

DESCRIPTION:
stolid; dull.

 ORIGIN: *1810–20; < Late Latin*

"It developed that the bovine Mrs.
Levy and the tell-tale Mrs. Levine
had gone back that morning."

145

defile

[dih-fahyl]

verb

DESCRIPTION:
to make foul, dirty, or unclean;
pollute; taint; debase.

ORIGIN: *1275–1325; Middle English*

"I felt that to seek her presence
would be almost to defile her."

repudiate

[ri-pyoo-dee-eyt]

verb

DESCRIPTION:
to reject with disapproval
or condemnation

ORIGIN: *1535–45; < Latin*

*"He was about to repudiate the idea
scornfully, when he sneezed!"*

dissipated

[dis-uh-pey-tid]

adjective

DESCRIPTION:
indulging in or characterized by
excessive devotion to pleasure

ORIGIN: *First recorded in 1600–10*

"Wild, dissipated, reckless, he was
dismissed immediately."

squealer

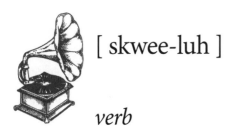

[skwee-luh]

verb

DESCRIPTION:
to turn informer; inform.

 ORIGIN: *C13 squelen, of imitative origin*

Tyrãnis lu
di magiftro
rum.

"I know a boy's code of honor, and
how he regards a 'squealer.'"

lingerer

 [lin-geruh]

verb

DESCRIPTION:
to remain or stay on in a place
longer than is usual or expected

 ORIGIN: *1250–1300; Middle English*

"We lingered awhile after the party."

highfaluting

[hahy-fuh-loot-n]

adjective

DESCRIPTION:
pompous; bombastic;
haughty; pretentious.

ORIGIN: *1830–40; high + falutin
(perhaps orig. flutin, variant of
fluting, present participle of flute)*

"He's got to give up this highfaluting nonsense
of his if he expects me to support him."

carious

[kair-ee-uh_s]

adjective

DESCRIPTION:
having caries, as teeth; decayed.

ORIGIN: *1520–30; < Latin*

"She is very charming, no doubt; but look
at her mouth, and you will see she has
carious teeth—des dents Carrier!"

blench

[blench]

verb

DESCRIPTION:
to shrink; flinch; quail:

ORIGIN: *before 1000; Middle English blenchen, Old English blencan; cognate with Old Norse blekkja, Middle High German blenken*

"If that ye stammer or blench, or anyways boggle at the swearing, he will not believe you; and by the mass, he shall die."

egregious

[ih-gree-juh_s, -jee-uh_s]

adjective

DESCRIPTION:
extraordinary in some bad
way; glaring; flagrant:

ORIGIN: *1525–35; < Latin*

"By Hugo's brother I will be tried on no
charge;—seeing that he is, was, and ever will
be—in charity I speak it—an egregious fool."

trite

[trahyt]

adjective

DESCRIPTION:
lacking in freshness or effectiveness
because of constant use or excessive
repetition; hackneyed; stale:

ORIGIN: *1540–50; < Latin*

"There is a trite proverb to the effect that
the proof of the pudding is in the eating."

periphrastic

[per-uh-fras-tik]

adjective

DESCRIPTION:
word; circumlocutory; roundabout.

ORIGIN: *1795–1805; < Greek*

"Periphrastic epithets are part of the original and common stock of the Teutonic poetry." **167**

garish

[gair-ish, gar-]

adjective

DESCRIPTION:
crudely or tastelessly colorful, showy,
or elaborate, as clothes or decoration.

ORIGIN: *1535–45; earlier gaurish, perhap:
equivalent to obsolete gaure to stare*

"It was horrible to have met this
garish embodiment of his past on the
very threshold of his fair future."

peacocky

[pee-kok-ee]

verb

DESCRIPTION:
to make a vainglorious display;
strut like a peacock.

ORIGIN: *1250–1300; Middle English*

"Raffish and peacocky, he lounged forward
to the window of the carriage."

risqué

[ri-skey]

adjective

DESCRIPTION:
daringly close to indelicacy or
impropriety; off-color:

ORIGIN: *1865–70; < French, past
participle of risquer to risk*

"You can give Mrs. Blair all the risque Paris gossip at dinner."

quacksalver

[kwak-sal-ver]

noun

DESCRIPTION:
a charlatan.

ORIGIN: *1570–80; < early Dutch*

"Hugh could not help thinking there was more
or less of the quacksalver about the man."

surly

[sur-lee]

adjective

DESCRIPTION:
churlishly rude or bad-tempered

ORIGIN: *1560–70; spelling variant of obsolete sirly lordly, arrogant*

"Yes, we have breakfasted already,"
replied Mr. Wenzel, in a surly voice."

remonstrate

[ri-mon-streyt]

verb

DESCRIPTION:
to say or plead in protest,
objection, or disapproval.

ORIGIN: *1590–1600; < Medieval Latin*

"Whatever it might please those cruel
judges to inflict upon myself or Julia,—there
was none to remonstrate or interpose."

burble

[bur-buh_l]

verb

DESCRIPTION:
to speak in an excited manner; babble.

ORIGIN: *1275–1325; Middle English; perhaps variant of bubble*

"Meanwhile the author of the latest explanation
went from house to house to burble the news
in the company of his two witnesses."

repine

[ri-pahyn]

verb

DESCRIPTION:
to be fretfully discontented;
fret; complain.

ORIGIN: *First recorded in 1520–30*

"*"We must not repine,"* he wrote to his *wife on the 12th of October, the day after Hood sailed for England."*

taciturn

[tas-i-turn]

adjective

DESCRIPTION:
dour, stern, and silent in
expression and manner.

ORIGIN: *1765–75; < Latin*

"When I went up to the office where I was
o file, the door was open and the most
aciturn old man sat before a desk."

ratfink

[rat-fingk]

noun

DESCRIPTION:
a contemptible or thoroughly
unattractive person.

ORIGIN: *C20: from rat + fink*

"'Which one of you is the ratfink,"
came the harsh query."

varmint

[vahr-muh_nt]

noun

DESCRIPTION:
a despicable, obnoxious,
or annoying person.

ORIGIN: *1530–40; variant of vermin*

"I begun to fear that the varmint
had a cave, and so, cuss him!"

uptown

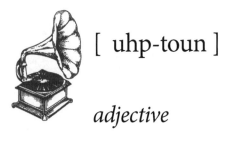

[uhp-toun]

adjective

DESCRIPTION:
characterized by or given to
pretentious or conspicuous show
in an attempt to impress others

ORIGIN: *First recorded in 1830–40;*

PAUL CLIFFORD

OR,

HURRAH FOR THE ROAD.

LONDON : E. LLOYD, SALISBURY-SQUARE, AND ALL BOOKSELLERS.

'There was an uptown pretension in the "get up" of this gentleman.'

191

peach

[peech]

verb

DESCRIPTION:
to inform against; betray.

ORIGIN: *1425–75; late Middle English peche*

"If her mother understood her
eagerness, she did not peach it, but
with Mr. Watkins it was different."

ignoble

[ig-noh-buhl]

adjective

DESCRIPTION:
of low character, aims, etc.; mean; base

ORIGIN: *1400–50; late Middle English*

"But I cannot think any save the most ignoble
criminals ever sat in a ducking-stool."

stoic

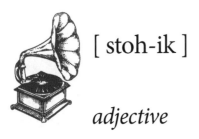

[stoh-ik]

adjective

DESCRIPTION:
displaying no emotional or
personal involvement

ORIGIN: *1350–1400; Middle English*

"His stoic air, his words of passive acceptance,
laid a calm upon the first outburst of bitter
grief from the two young creatures."

codger

[koj-er]

noun

DESCRIPTION:
an eccentric man, especially
one who is old.

ORIGIN: *1750–60; perhaps
variant of obsolete cadger*

""More easily said than done, old codger,"*
hiccoughed Robson, essaying to get
across the back of a restive mule."

scatterbrain

[skat-er-breyn]

noun

DESCRIPTION:
a person incapable of serious,
connected thought.

ORIGIN: *First recorded in
1780–90; scatter + brain*

"I'm such a scatterbrain - I'm always leaving my umbrella behind."

foozle

[foo-zuhl]

verb

DESCRIPTION:
to bungle; play clumsily:

ORIGIN: *First recorded in 1825–35; perhaps from dialectal German fuseln "to work badly, clumsily, hurriedly"*

"If I tried a trick out of turn, I
might foozle and lose prestige."

Printed in Great Britain
by Amazon